G IS FOR GOLAZO
THE ULTIMATE SOCCER ALPHABET

CHRISTIAN PULISIC

WORDS BY
JAMES LITTLEJOHN

ILLUSTRATIONS BY
MATTHEW SHIP LEY

HOMARE SAWA

ABBY WAMBACH

CHRISTINE SINCLAIR

To the kid reading this who will one day
be the face of their own letter. — J.L.

To Elise, I scored when I married you. — M.S.

Library of Congress Cataloging-in-Publication Data available upon request.

This book is available in quantity at special discounts for your group or organization. For further information, contact:
Triumph Books LLC, 814 North Franklin Street, Chicago, Illinois 60610
(312) 337-0747
www.triumphbooks.com

Printed in USA
ISBN: 978-1-62937-671-4

A IS FOR ARROW

In the 1950s, Alfredo Di Stéfano
— Real Madrid's "Blond Arrow" —
shot to the top of the game.

ZLATAN IBRAHIMOVIC

B IS FOR BICYCLE KICK

Gear up and get ready to fly. Bicycle kicks are one of the most difficult — and thrilling — plays in all of sports.

KLAUS FISCHER

LEÔNIDAS DA SILVA

C IS FOR CANNON

Boom! With his long-range firepower, Gareth Bale's
left leg is more like a cannon.

D IS FOR DERBY

No matter where you are or what you call it, Derby or Clásico, beating your rival always means more.

HARRY KANE

THIERRY HENRY

THE NORTH LONDON DERBY
ARSENAL VS. TOTTENHAM

E IS FOR ELEPHANTS

Charge! The world's fastest herd of èlèphants plays for the Ivory Coast.

DIDIER DROGBA

F IS FOR FOX IN THE BOX

Beware the fox in the box. These predatory goal poachers are always ready to pounce.

JAMIE VARDY

G IS FOR GOOOOOOOOOOOOAAA

Every goal counts the same...

LIONEL MESSI

AAAAAAAAAAALLLLLLLLLLLL!

but it takes extra style and skill to score a ¡GOLAZO!

CRISTIANO RONALDO

H IS FOR HAND OF GOD

It shouldn't have counted but can never be forgotten. In the '86 World Cup, Argentina's Diego Maradona infamously scored "a little with the head" and "a little with the hand of God."

I IS FOR ILLUSIONIST

Now you see it, now you don't. Andrés "The Illusionist" Iniesta's magical misdirections left crowds wondering: "How'd he do that?"

J IS FOR JUGGLING

Creative as they come, the juggling genius
Ronaldinho was one of Brazil's most
entertaining exports.

K IS FOR KING

Long live the king. Born Edson Arantes do Nascimento, Pelé would go on to score an unbelievable 1,281 goals across a career that has no comparison.

L IS FOR LIONS

All of England has obsessed over its team, the Three Lions, since their debut in 1872 — the year they played in the first international match in the history of football.

SIR STANLEY MATTHEWS

M IS FOR MAESTRO

The maestro in the midfield. Andrea Pirlo made music on the pitch as he set the tempo and orchestrated his team's attack.

N IS FOR NUTMEG

Why go around your foe when another way is more fun?
Dribbling between their legs is how a nutmeg is done.

RONALDO "THE PHENOMENON"

O IS FOR ORANGE

If you ain't Dutch, you ain't much. Johan Cruyff and the Oranje made total football famous in the '70s.

P IS FOR PONYTAIL

Italian legend Roberto Baggio's play was simply divine… and so was his mane.

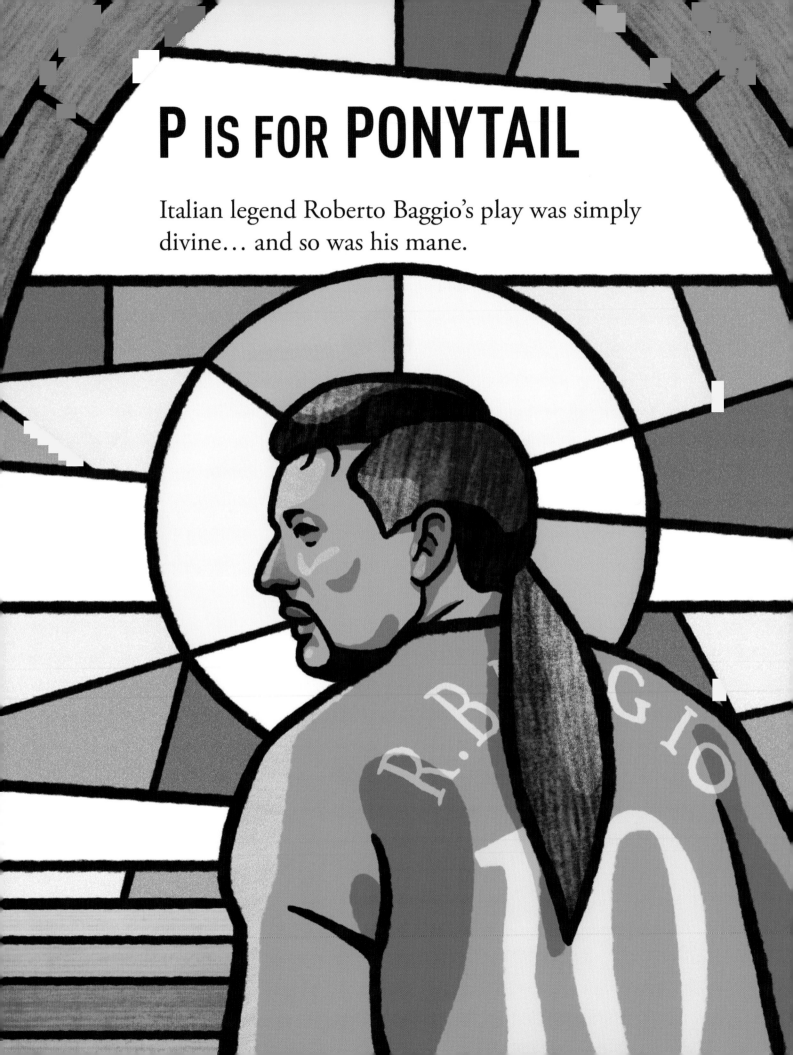

Q IS FOR QUEEN

Marta, the quick-footed queen of football, has been named the world's best more than any other woman.

R IS FOR RAINBOW

Neymar's bag of tricks includes arcing rainbow kicks —
one of the rarest, most colorful moves you'll ever see.

S IS FOR SOCCEROO

Down Under there's a land full of kangaroos.
When they're hopping down the pitch, they
call 'em Socceroos.

TIM CAHILL

T IS FOR TRACTOR

Powerful, tireless, and determined, Javier Zanetti's impressive motor earned him the nickname "El Tractor."

U IS FOR USA

Love for the game is growing in the United States, home of Mia Hamm, Alex Morgan, and the world's most successful women's team.

V IS FOR VUVUZELA

Played loud and proud in South Africa, the vuvuzela is the horn heard round the world.

DAVID BECKHAM

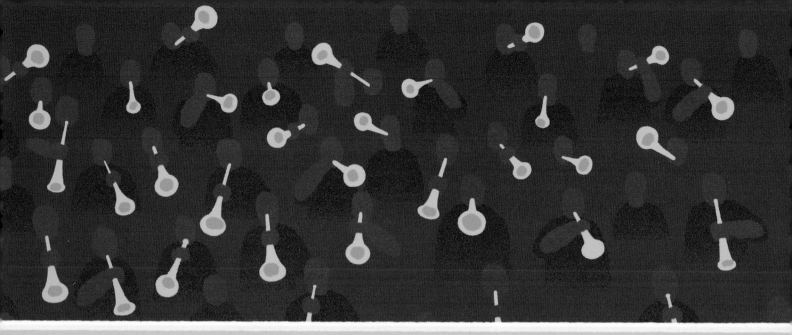

W IS FOR WONDERGOALS OVER WALLS

No wall can stop a swerving, curving, spectacular set piece.

X IS FOR XI

Every player, at every level, strives to take their place in the starting eleven.

"SUPERMAN"
GIGI BUFFON

"THE CAPTAIN"
PAOLO MALDINI

"THE EMPEROR"
FRANZ BECKENBAUER

"THE COMMUTER"
CAFU

STEVEN GERRARD

"THE OCTOPUS"
PAUL POGBA

"THE 5TH BEATLE"
GEORGE BEST

BOBBY CHARLTON

"PHARAOH"
MO SALAH

XAVI
"THE PUPPET MASTER"

"THE KID"
CARLOS VALDERRAMA

Y IS FOR YELLOW CARD

One yellow, two yellows, three yellows, four... Sergio Ramos has been booked a couple hundred times more.

Z IS FOR ZIZOU IN ZEBRA STRIPES

Before making his mark in Madrid, the legendary Zinedine "Zizou" Zidane sported the black and white of Juventus.

IL GLADIATORE

FRANCESCO TOTTI

THE END